Yog[a]

The Ultimate Guide to Mastering Yoga for Beginners!

Check out what others have been saying about this book.....

"With this book it's been Easier Than ever to begin successfully practicing Yoga on a daily basis and it's so much fun!"

   - **Jason Thompson**

"After reading this book I've finally completed my Yoga Session and I feel so amazing!"

   - ***Bree Paradise***

"This was the best book on Yoga I've read in a long time. It's a pretty simple book but really sums everything up. Thank You!"

   - **Michelle Tarter**

Table of Contents

Introduction

Chapter 1 - Yoga: The Science of Life

Chapter 2- Styles and Types of Yoga

Chapter 3- Tips for a Yoga Newbie

Chapter 4- Combat the Excuses

Chapter 5- Basic Poses

Conclusion

Bonus Chapter: Zen for Beginners

Valerie Sandston **Copyright © 2015**

All rights reserved. No part of this book may be reproduced in any form without permission in writing from the author. Reviewers may quote brief passages in reviews.

Disclaimer

No part of this publication may be reproduced or transmitted in any form or by any means, mechanical or electronic, including photocopying or recording, or by any information storage and retrieval system, or transmitted by email without permission in writing from the publisher.

While all attempts and efforts have been made to verify the information held within this publication, neither the author nor the publisher assumes any responsibility for errors, omissions, or opposing interpretations of the content herein.

This book is for entertainment purposes only. The views expressed are those of the author alone, and should not be taken as expert instruction or commands. The reader of this book is responsible for his or her own actions when it comes to reading the book.

Adherence to all applicable laws and regulations, including international, federal, state, and local governing professional licensing, business practices, advertising, and all other aspects of doing business in the US, Canada, or any other jurisdiction is the sole responsibility of the purchaser or reader.

Neither the author nor the publisher assumes any responsibility or liability whatsoever on the behalf of the purchaser or reader of these materials.

Any received slight of any individual or organization is purely unintentional.

Introduction

I want to thank you and congratulate you for downloading the book, **"Yoga: The Ultimate Guide to Mastering Yoga for Beginners!"**

This book contains proven steps and strategies for mastering the art of Yoga and further understanding its essence, procedures and benefits.

Considered the most diversified practice in the world, Yoga offers a myriad of health benefits and is becoming the new fitness method. Moreover, the practice continues to spread its peace and message all over the world. By practicing yoga regularly, you will be amazed on how it can turn you to a better, healthier and peaceful version of you. This book aims to help you get started practicing yoga and incorporating its disciplines in your daily routine. Likewise, the book will teach you some of the basic poses for beginners and how to overcome the common excuses and misconceptions of this renowned activity.

Enhance the quality of your life and achieve a new level of self-enlightenment with the help of yoga!

Thanks again for downloading this book, I hope you enjoy it!

Chapter 1

Yoga: The Science of Life

Whenever someone mentions yoga, most people would imagine a person, Indian-sitting in a poor lit room, with lighted candles and chanting "ohm" repetitively. But what most of us didn't know is that yoga is the science of life, an ancient art that is present for thousands of centuries. It is a Sanskrit word which means "unite" or "join". The recent years has raised its popularity as an efficient way to bring back the balance in a person's mental, physical, spiritual and emotional state.

Evolved in what is called "sat yuga" (golden age), people who seek for eternal truth has developed yoga, aiming to answer the question, "Who am I?" which has pondered since time immemorial.

THE GOAL OF EVERY PRACTITIONER

The fundamental goal of a yogi (a person proficient in yoga), is to attain pure spirit, find absolute freedom from pain and find an inner peace. Yogis see beautiful things that are actually difficult to describe such as people who are more relaxed, faces soften, happier state and fallen defenses. The myriad of health benefits that a person can obtain from practicing yoga has made it more popular with professionals, young adults, working parent, entrepreneurs and students among others. Even celebrities and sports athletes are fond of attending yoga classes. Before you start to try yoga, below are some pointers that a beginner like you must know.

Not just by doing poses will you be considered yogi

Yoga's inspiration and beauty is that it includes various elements. While most of us are only familiar with yoga's physical aspects, practicing the asana (posture in performing the hatha yoga) is only at the top of it. You should have a more in-depth, more love and more spirit in understanding yoga aside from being on the mat. There are many things to learn and as a yogi, you should figure it out.

Honor the present moment regardless what it is-

Like any other practice, yoga can be hard or at ease. There will be times that you wanted to run out of the room or no longer can hold on

to a position the teacher teach you. Whatever it is, you must acknowledge it. Yoga offers us the opportunity to be present and get rid of foreign thoughts and stories in our minds. This may sound easy but this is actually the most difficult part of the practice.

Don't just do it, feel it

When you are on the mat make sure to feel your poses and not just perform it. This is similar when a dancer or a ballerina feels every pose, every step and turn of the dance. Arch your back, feel your heart and do what the practice told you to do. Don't mind how others look at it. Focus on how you feel every pose and the beauty of it. There are others, who perform for the sake of performing in a crowd and making sure that everyone is watching. This can be annoying especially for those who fully embrace the art of yoga. Better watch what is happening in your mind and not for other persons' approval if you are doing it right. Be present in the current situation so you feel the practice deep in your heart.

It is the practice for the "actual life"

More than just rolling down a mat in the studio next to a yogi, practicing the principles of yoga must be applied in the outside world. This means staying present minded in the middle of an argument, at the office meeting, accepting things happening in the family and letting go of our ego. Take deep breaths whenever you feel angry and defensive. This will help you to stay calm, keep on track and negotiate peacefully. It is a win-win situation that people around you will gain benefit as well.

How you react on things while you are on the mat is the reflection of how you react in real-life scenarios

More often, something really challenging abruptly comes up while doing your poses. Beginners usually experience the feeling of wanting to run out of the room when they no longer get hold of a pose. This reflects their defense mechanisms and reactions in life. Self-doubt is a common distraction that is actually happening on the mat and outside the studio. Believe in yourself and practice real hard.

Remember, yoga is not just a mere practice or activity that you should do. It is a way of living and a practice of balance that we can actually apply on a daily basis. Let the art of yoga transform you by being willing to be present minded every moment. It is a science that offers many health benefits and happiness. More than just clearing our minds, it also teaches us how to effectively deal with real life problems and to face what is inevitable. Anyone can do it with the right attitude.

Chapter 2

Styles and Types of Yoga for Beginners

If you are a newbie to yoga, there are plenty of options for types of yoga for you. Any style can help you improve your flexibility, strength and balance. Likewise, it will help you release the tension in your body, to make you relax and quiet the mind. In general, yoga offers a whole range of holistic approach for the body's overall well-being.

Hence, to acquire the most benefit, one should choose a style that matches their fitness level, personality and objectives for practicing yoga.

YOGA STYLES

There are many different styles of yoga and you need to choose first, the type that suits your interest and needs. While there is a long list of yoga style you can choose from, below are some of the commonly practiced.

Basically almost all yoga styles emerged from India and are practiced all over the world. However, new variations of yoga such as the laughter yoga are not included in the traditional style. Nonetheless, these practices were built around the principles of yoga and aim to aid people to obtain permanent inner peace. Below are some of the popular variations of yoga;

Vinyasa yoga is one of the popular styles. It means "sequence" and its practitioners move through one pose after the other. In vinyasa, you will learn how to control your breath properly while moving and doing a sequence of movement. Vinyasa develops the rhythm of breathing. This is usually practiced in Western countries. This is a continuous and almost dance-like movement and not just the usual posing and stretching. The teacher can alter the sequence and postures depending on the practitioner's level.

Ashtanga Vinyasa Yoga is another type of yoga that is physically demanding and can be best practice by persons who are athletic and reasonably fit. However, there are classes for beginners that you can try to determine if this type will suit you. It is a system of breathing and movement where every movement is incorporated with postures and inhale or exhale. It is traditionally taught using the "Mysore" style where its practitioners are working on their own pace with the guidance of a teacher. It allows beginners to practice together with the advanced practitioners. The Ashtanga yoga has 6-series with set of postures that cannot be interchanged which aim to enhance one's breathing and movement. It also heats the body which purifies the organs, the blood and nervous system.

Bikram Yoga is a modern version of Hatha Yoga that was established during the 1970s. Its classes follow the same format of the traditional Hatha with the same postures and two breathing exercises that last to 90 minutes. Only certified teachers of Bikram can teach this. One of its prominent features is that, it is performed in a heated room same as with the Hot Yoga.

Yengar Yoga is a style that utilizes props in performing asanas. Yogacharya B.K.S. Iyengar developed this style based on Sage Patanjali's yoga principles. The usual props used are wooden blocks, blankets, straps, benches, chairs, sandbags, pillows and bolsters. This style is ideal and safe for beginners and advanced practitioners alike. The props are helping the body to attain a pose's ideal alignment and make the asana easier for students to perform. Likewise, this yoga style is recommended for sick and tired persons at home.

Hot Yoga classes that are generic are not the same with Bikram Yoga although they share numerous features. Unlike the Bikram where a sequence must be strictly followed, the postures in Hot Yoga classes can be changed based on the studio where it is practiced. Usually, its classes are performed in a heated room (105°F) and with 40% humidity. This is not the type of yoga that everyone enjoys. This is a demanding and very sweaty practice which is not suitable for pregnant women. Among its benefits are mind clarity and balancing the emotions.

Hatha Yoga generally refers to a yoga class that incorporated meditation, Pranyama (breathing techniques) and Asana or postures. It moves at a slow pace which makes it ideal for beginners. The classes vary based on the teacher's approach to Yoga. Moreover, Hatha Yoga is good for injured or unwell persons to help them recover faster.

Kripalu Yoga is a variation of Hatha Yoga which is less physical and gentler. It involves a lot of meditation, breathing work and awakening the body, mind and spiritual awareness. It also promotes emotional well-being and healing. However, this is considered a challenging yoga as it aims to transform the lives of its practitioners.

MASTERING YOGA POSES

To master various yoga poses, you should have the will power, must be physically fit and flexible and have a regular practice. As a beginner, you must understand that your body is unique and has a different ability compared to other people. You can master any pose by being dedicated to practice it.

Practice the pose by holding onto it for at least 10 seconds or depending on your strength. Practice every pose within your body's limits as performing a pose while stretching beyond the body's ability can cause injury. Stretch until you start to feel pain. Repeat the asana based on your body's ability and gradually increase its duration. Most important, do not compare your pace, your body's ability and yourself with other practitioners both beginners and advanced. Let your body adjust to this practice and totally embrace its principles.

Remember that nobody becomes expert on a certain thing overnight. Start today and stop worrying if you can perform Yoga better. You will eventually find an efficient way to achieve better mental and physical health.

Furthermore, yoga is more than just asanas (postures). There are also classes that cover pranayama (breath work) and meditation.

THE 6 BRANCHES OF YOGA

During the ancient times, the practice of yoga was usually referred to as a living entity such as a tree with branches, roots and fruits. One of the 6 branches is the Hatha Yoga. Each of the branches represents certain way of life with their unique functions and characteristics. Some person finds a specific branch more inviting than the others however, the participation in one of these branches does not hinder a person to participate in another. More likely you will find these paths overlapping naturally.

RAJA YOGA – meditation is the focus of this yoga which attracts introvert people. This branch's approach is to strictly cohere to yoga's eight limbs in order; ethical standards, self-discipline, posture, breathe control, sensory withdrawal, concentration, meditation and final liberation.

KARMA YOGA – is the path of service that no one of us can escape. Its principle is that, what we are experiencing today is a result of our actions in the past. With this in mind, our present efforts to being unselfish and negative would create a future that is free from all undesirable conditions and feelings.

BHAKTI YOGA- refers to the path of devotion. Its principle is to see the divine in every creation. Likewise, it promotes positive emotions and to cultivate tolerance and acceptance for everyone. Martin Luther King, Jr., Mother Teresa and Mahatma Gandhi are some of the prominent bhakti yogis in history.

JNANA YOGA –this is the yoga of wisdom, the mind and the path of scholar. It requires the maturity of the intellect by studying texts and scriptures of the yogic tradition. Its approach is the most direct and at the same time, the most difficult. It requires serious study and appeals to people who are intellectually inclined.

TANTRA YOGA- the 6th branch of yoga and the most misunderstand one. It is the ritual's pathways which include the sanctity of sexuality. Among the major branches, this is the most obscure and usually appeals to those who relate with the principles of feminine and enjoys ceremony. Likewise, if you are moved by the importance of rituals and celebrations and find magic in it, this yoga can be the right one for you.

ASHTANGA YOGA- this is the most popular among all the branches of yoga and is widely practiced nowadays. Literally, ashtanga mean 8 limbs. The limbs basically serve as guidelines on the purpose of life and how to meaningfully live it. It also acts as prescription for ethical conduct and moral as well as self-discipline.

Now that you already know the types of yoga and its basic principles, it's time to get ready and prepare for the whole new environment.

Chapter 3

Tips for a Yoga Newbie

Regardless if you are just starting with yoga at home or in a class and instructor, you can learn the basics of yoga in various ways. A good instructor is always the first bet of course but if it's not possible, there are several yoga books, training videos, audio tapes, CD and DVD and websites you can learn and understand yoga. Likewise, there are a host of Yoga teachers offering classes in offices, halls, private studios and even schools that aim to cater the needs of both sexes. Yoga classes are also available now online. And because yoga can be demanding, you must further understand its principles as well as your body's ability.

- Yoga can be energizing, slow or gentle, invigorating, technical or demanding or most of the times, a combination of these qualities. Each style has its own methods and takes on philosophy and practitioners can base their preferences on it.

- As a beginner, you may practice yoga for at least 15-20 minutes in your first week. As you progress, you can do it for 30-40 minutes and learn new poses. Increase your duration later on to 1 1/2 hours for best results.

- You can practice yoga at anytime of the day that is convenient for you but you should not have eaten any foods for at least 3 hours. Preferably, do it at the same time each day so it will become a habit.

- Practicing yoga in the morning and evening is better so there will be fewer distractions especially if you are doing it at home. Doing it in the morning will keep you energetic and alert for the entire day's activities. If you'll do it in the evening, it helps you reduce stress, feel relax and calm the mind that promotes a good night sleep.

- Doing it a home with the help of instructional CDs or online will give you the chance to do it with family and group of friends. If you prefer doing it in a studio, you can work with other students and learn new tips and poses with the help of a teacher.

- It is ideal to practice yoga in open spaces such as balcony or terrace. If doing it in a room, make sure that it is free from clutter and furniture, free from noise and with fresh air for more comfort.

- For beginners, the most important focus is mastering the poses while breathing correctly. This sounds simple to others but it takes more concentration to keep aware of the positions of the arms, core, back, legs, hands, feet and head while breathing deeply.

- Practicing yoga poses is considered an exercise and doing it improperly may lead to injury. You should have a clear sense of what are your limits and the right pace to master every pose.

- Moreover, yoga isn't a competition so take your time to master every poses. Listen to your body - pain and tightness means you need to warm up more, skip a day of practice or modify your pose. A thorough warm-up is ideal so look for a class that has it.

- Before joining any kind of activity or exercise, better to consult your doctor first to determine any medical condition that might be compromised in safely practicing yoga.

- Wear clothes that are comfortable and not too tight so you can gracefully perform the poses without yanking up your shirt or minding your baggy pants and getting conscious on how you look.

- Although water is not necessary for most yoga classes (except from hot yoga), still come hydrated. Don't eat at least for 2 hours before you practice as bendy shapes can affect how you feel in the inside.

- Yoga isn't just about those bendy shapes but it's about being fit and strong. It is about being in the present by listening to our own breath. Likewise, never push too much into pain. If it doesn't feel right or it hurts you, tell the teacher. Be truthful to your body and how it feels. You may want to be gentle and kind to yourself and not abuse your body.

- Don't mind other people in the room during the practice. They don't really care how you look, what are you wearing or if you look funny doing a pose. Focus on your breathing. Your mind should be steer clear of foreign thoughts or else, you will never do the poses successfully. Listen to your breathe and be present at the moment.

- Whilst there can be talk about the Divine or God, yoga is not a type of religion. It doesn't force you to believe in anything but it's about the experience. Learn the postures, practice breathing, meditate and give yourself a treat by harvesting the benefits it offers. Yoga is also a tool to enhance whatever your religious beliefs are through body-mind awareness.

- Concentrate and be conscientious on what you are doing on your mat. Don't talk while exercising and focus on your position and breathe. If possible stay away from all distractions especially if you're doing it at home.

- Your breathing is an important aspect of yoga. Breathe deeply and slowly and use your nose breathing in and out.

- Never practice yoga if you are under the influence of alcohol. Likewise, you don't have to totally give up smoking or become a vegetarian before you start practicing yoga. Yoga can aid you to overcome those bad habits and bring alignment in your spiritual aspect to overcome those vices you wanted to get rid of.

- be mindful of the space around you as yoga classes tend to be packed out. Leave enough space for other students and yourself. Respect and be aware of the space to avoid injuries as well when you topple from a certain pose.

- You must invest on a good mat. Whilst plastic vinyl and PVC are widely use in most yoga mats, there are new and safe options flourishing the marketplace. There are yoga mats made of dried grass, natural rubber, organic cotton and biodegradable compounds. Whatever your preference is, invest in purchasing a good mat since it is the most important tool you'll use during class.

Do not feel bad if the instructor or teacher will correct you as it is the best way for you to learn. Avoid judging yourself as well or compare to what other students are doing. Keep thing light-hearted and enjoy yourself on the mat. It is an individual process so trust your own judgement on what you can do. Over time, you will get to know the difference of being afraid to do something over what is impossible or harmful to do. There's no need to rush as your body knows its limit and capacity.

Why Practice Yoga

Yoga is good for our cardiovascular health. It also develops strength and flexibility as well as mental clarity and emotional balance. This is safe for all ages and even those with injuries or sick can modify yoga to suit them. It initiates healing from within and a good way to create wellness. Moreover, it is a form of practice that will give you overall benefits: strength, flexibility, balance, endurance and relaxation. Hence, the ultimate challenge of the body and mind.

The different positions in yoga exercise our different ligaments and tendons. If you live a sedentary life, yoga can help you become flexible. You can attained it easily specifically on parts that that are not consciously worked out in other types of activity.

More than just exercising our joints, stretching our body and releasing our tensions, yoga can also massage our internal organs in a thorough manner. It massages and stimulate the organs in a wholesome way especially those that are hardly stimulated such as the prostate. This act provides nourishment while flushing out toxins out of the body.

Nonetheless, yoga is an overall health and fitness practice that not only targets our physical aspects but also touches our spiritual and mental areas. Through meditation, we can all harmonize our mind and body. It helps achieve an emotional balance by creating conditions that would make us unaffected in our surroundings. In turn, we will be able to develop positive outlook in life.

Chapter 4

Combat the Excuses

As a beginner, you will be eventually hearing and feeling many excuses from practicing yoga. These excuses might scare away a person who would want to try yoga but remember, regular practice can make these doubts and fears go away. Below are some of the common excuses and why and how to overcome them.

I am too busy!

This is the main reason why you should try practicing yoga. A person who is living a busy life and is always on the go usually neglects their overall health. With yoga, you can expand and extend the time. It is an antidote enabling you to somehow move in a slow pace. You can always find time for this very essential activity. Turn off the T.V or your gadgets, get up earlier than the usual, and use your lunch hour to do some poses or skip the evening football game. 10-20 minutes is all that it takes everyday to practice yoga and start making a big difference.

I'm not flexible for this.

This is the primary concern of many beginners who are afraid of those bendy yogis and aching muscles after every practice. They usually think to themselves that they can never do such poses perfectly. Regardless how inflexible a person is, by consistently practicing yoga, that person can develop flexibility and could do things beyond their expectations. Patience and dedication are the great combination to finally touch your toes (Forward Fold) or reach your ankles (Bow Pose) again.

It is intimidating.

It is normal for first-timers to somehow feel intimidated and terrified on going to their very first yoga class with other students practicing yoga. We would think if others would laugh at us secretly as we try to do a pose or who's watching us but in reality, this is not the case. Your fellow students are really into their own practices and focusing on what they are doing. The advanced students are more concentrated in achieving the deepest place possible from within. Moreover, most of the yogis are friendly and very supportive especially to a beginner like you.

I am too old to learn this.

Most people believe that given their age, it was too late for them to try out yoga, however, the principles of yoga and its practices target everyone regardless of their age. There are yoga classes for adults that honor more of the body due to some limitations, health concerns and balance issues because of aging. Moreover, poses are modified for adults and the pace is slower. These types of yoga classes prioritize safety, alignment and self-pacing especially for the elder students. Yoga is apparently not only for the young people. The poses can be changed based on the students' capabilities and limitations.

I have many health issues and injuries.

What most of didn't know is that there are various yoga programs nowadays that are specifically designed for health conditions such as cancer, stress chronic illnesses and insomnia. It is best to get an advised from your health care provider to do some modification on the yoga class you would like to attend. Eventually, yoga is for everyone and sickness and injuries shouldn't be an excuse.

I don't fit in the profile of a typical yogi.

If your main concern is that you don't look like a yogi, have no fear. Whether you are a smoker, a junk food lover or an alcohol drinker, there are various yoga classes tailored fit for you. Yoga also increases its popularity among male. Release the myth of not being fit for the profile and start practicing yoga.

Yoga classes are expensive.

In reality, there are various ways to make yoga classes affordable for you. Despite the high prices that some yoga instructor and yoga studios initiate, there are community based yoga classes and free online instructional videos you can get advantage of. Other options include fitness center membership or local yoga studios that offer discounts and can be paid on a monthly basis.

There are several things that would be holding us from practicing yoga and reaping the myriad of benefits it offers. We generate plenty of excuses that actually hinder us from committing ourselves or even trying yoga in the first place. Don't allow these excuses to derail from practicing yoga and enhancing your overall well being.

Moreover, attending your first yoga class can be intimidating since everybody else looks relax and confident of themselves. They are all fitter, stronger, bendy and leaner but remember, every single person in that class including the teacher was once a beginner. It is their regular practice and dedication to learn is what makes them the person you are seeing, stronger and healthier. You too can achieve those attributes.

Chapter 5

Basic Poses

There are various reasons why adding yoga to your daily routine is healthy and beneficial. It improves flexibility; helps tone the muscles, enhance your balance and reduce your stress. Now that you are ready to give it a try, below are beginner poses also known as asanas for you to master.

SUKHASANA (Easy Cross Leg)

On a yoga mat, sit cross legged with your palms up, hand on your knees. Keep the spine straight while pushing the bones down on the floor or in yoga-speak, "sit bones". Keep your eyes closed and inhale. According to yoga experts, this is an ideal pose for beginners to do an assessment. Sitting on the floor allows you to feel and see the legs' external rotation. It is also good to relive stress and boosts the flexibility of your back.

MARJARYASANA/BITALASANA (Cat-Cow Pose)

Get on the mat with your hands below your shoulders and knees below your hips. Equally distribute your weight on both hands and spread the fingers wide. Inhale and arch your back as you begin to lower your chin down to your chest. Exhale and lower your back to a scoop shape while you lift your head then tilt it back. This is good to address back pain and loosen the spine.

VRKASASANA (Tree Pose)

Begin by standing straight. Bring both the hands in a prayer position and life it over the head. Bend your left knee to the left side, press the left foot to your inner thigh while keeping you balance on your right leg. Hold this pose for 30 seconds then switch legs. It helps the body to stretch longer and also improves flexibility and balance. Apparently, the challenge here is to keep your balance in one leg. Poor balance is usually the result of a distracted mind. Moreover, this pose helps strengthen the claves, spine, ankles and thighs. It also helps reduce flat feet and stretches the shoulders and inner thighs.

BADDHA KONASANA (Bound Angle/Cobbler Pose) - is a usual sitting position of Indian cobblers. It improves general circulation by stimulating the heart. It also alleviates stress, anxiety, mild depression and fatigue. Sit straight while your legs are out in front. Bend your knees while pulling your heels toward the pelvis as you exhale. Drop your knees to the side and press your feet's soles. Do not force your knees. Stay in this pose for about 5 minutes then inhale. Lift your legs slowly away from the floor and go back to the original pose.

ADHO MUKHA SVANASANA (Downward Facing Dog Pose)

Form your body to an inverted V-shape. Begin by placing the hands in front of you, palms down in your mat. It should be slightly in front of the shoulders. Put your knees on the ground under the hips. Lift your knees as you exhale and lift your hips and buttocks toward the ceiling. As you push your thighs back, stretch the heels toward the floor. Keep the head down between and inline the upper arms. You should be able to create a long spine. Likewise, this pose is a resting pose and the usual pose introduced to beginners. This also alleviates menopausal symptoms as well as menstrual discomfort.

BALASANA (Child's Pose)

Among the yoga poses, experts agreed that this is the most healing. The fetal position will make you feel relax. From the downward-facing dog pose, bend your knees while bringing your chest towards the floor. Lower the head and shoulders to the floor as well. Place both arms on your sides and palms up. Breathe in as you relax. This is an ideal post to stretch the back and release tensions.

TADASANA (Mountain Pose)

This pose is very simple as all you have to do is stand still with your hands broad at your side and your chest open. Feel the sensations in your back and legs and on your feet on the floor. It helps correct your posture, strengthen the thighs and feet and tone the muscles around the abdomen. Likewise, the mountain pose helps clear the mind, improves stability and balance.

There are other asanas that you can practice once you mastered these basic steps. Keep in mind that doing these poses should be comfortable for you or else, don't do it. Stop if it's painful and respect your body's limitations. The practice of yoga should be a pleasurable experience, not an excruciating one.

Conclusion

Thank you again for downloading this book!

I hope this book was able to help you to get started practicing yoga.

The next step is to determine which type of yoga suits your personality and interests' best. After that, start initiating yoga into your daily routine no matter how busy you are. Make time to do yoga to achieve utmost state of well-being as well as having spiritual connection from deep within. Perform the exercises discussed above whenever you got the chance. You don't need to force yourself to do it if there's pain. Listen to your body, focus with your breathing, don't mind others and feel the present moment.

Yoga offers countless of benefits that we all can take advantage of. Help others to become a better person by sharing them your knowledge and experience about yoga.

Finally, if you enjoyed this book, please take the time to share your thoughts and post a review on Amazon. It'd be greatly appreciated!

Thank you and good luck!

Bonus Chapter: Zen for Beginners

Reiki is the accent art of healing by using the laying on of hands. The person who is administering the healing becomes a vessel for the healing energy addressing physical, mental, emotional and spiritual issues that the recipient is dealing with.

Before we go any further, I want to explain that this can be very dangerous for the person practicing Reiki. When you practice Reiki you have to open yourself up to the healing energies. This can also open you up to many other energies as well. Those who are not experienced can allow negative energies to come into them and although this will not harm the recipient it has been known to cause many issues in the person who is practicing's life.

Many people will tell you that you do not have to worry about protecting yourself when you are practicing but that you need to make sure you are balance. While I do believe that it is very important to be balanced within oneself when practicing Reiki, I also believe it is important to set up a barrier so that if any negative energy were trying to come your way you would be safe from any harm.

It is just like when a psychic prepares for a session, they know they are going to encounter good but on the off chance any negative comes their way the prepare for it beforehand. You can choose not to protect yourself and that is completely up to you but this next little bit is for those who would like some protection.

The first thing you need to do is choose a spiritual path and follow it. I am not going to get into a discussion on the different paths and opinions on each but you have to understand that Reiki is a very spiritual process therefore you need to ground yourself in a spiritual belief. This does not mean that you have to become a saint over night, what it means is that you try.

Once you have chosen a spiritual path you are going to pray for protection from every negative energy that would try to come against you. While you are healing, if you feel anything negative coming toward you, you should focus on a sacred object from whatever spiritual path you have chosen.

Finally after the session is over you need to break all ties with any negative energy that may have come upon you.

Many people who practice Reiki inadvertently take on the issues of the person they are healing so if you are healing someone with a mental disorder you need to physically speak out that you break any ties with mental disorders and you do not allow them in your life.

It may seem a little strange at first but you will get used to speaking these things out. And since you are practicing Reiki to begin with you probably already understand they type of havoc negative energy can wreak on a persons life.

You also need to understand that you do not control the healing Reiki energy. Therefore you are going to be unable to tell someone you are going to help them with a specific issue. You see, a person may come to you with a physical issue or you may try to heal yourself of a specific physical issue only to find that it has not been affected. The Reiki energy goes to where it is need most in the body, bringing complete balance.

So if you are going to practice Reiki you need to explain to people that you cannot heal a specific problem but the Reiki energy will heal what is needed the most. It works like this, if someone came into my home and stated that they needed physical healing because they were always tired, the Reiki energy then finds that they are depressed therefore needing mental or emotional healing in order to bring balance to their lives. The Reiki energy would work on the depression and not the symptom of feeling tired.

Often times this discourages people but if it is explained beforehand they tend to be more accepting of the healing no matter what it is.

Before you can perform a Reiki session, you have to clear your own energy field. If you do not clear your own energy field, most of the energy that is channeled will go toward healing and cleansing your own energy field and not that of your client.

The most important thing you will ever learn from a Reiki class is that you are to work on yourself first. The fact is that those who care for others tend to avoid taking care of themselves. The first rule of Reiki is that if you do not take care of yourself first, you cannot take care of others.

You also need to understand that it is up to you to heal you as it is up to the client to heal themselves. You see if a client comes in asking you to heal them you need to explain to them that you are just a vessel for the energy, they will be harnessing that energy and actually doing the healing themselves.

You need to make sure that you do not just jump into giving others Reiki, this needs to be performed on yourself on a regular basis. The more you do it, the better you will get and the more in tune with the energy you will become. I suggest you actually give yourself Reiki for at least 3-4 months before ever practicing on someone else.

You also need to understand that you're body needs to be as healthy as possible to be the best Reiki provider. If you are not eating healthy foods, drinking a ton of sugary drinks, not exercising and just not taking care of your body you will not be very successful at Reiki.

You need to also focus on your mental, emotional and spiritual state as well as the environment you live in. If you live in a stressful environment and try to work Reiki on others, you will find that it does not work because the energy will again try to heal you first.

So make sure you are taking the time out to meditate, create a calm place at home as well as in the office if you begin using Reiki on others.

Now as I said you need to practice Reiki regularly to clear your own energy field. You need to do this daily and not just when you remember to.

To do self Reiki, you need to start with a relaxing environment. Most people prefer to practice self Reiki first thing in the morning when they wake up and in the evening when they are going to bed.

Make sure you have a calm, relaxing environment, you can also have a soothing recording that you listen to while you practice Reiki. Next you need to make sure you are in a comfortable position and have a set plan. You need to work down your plan in the same pattern every day. It will look something like this:

- *Top of Head*
- *Face*

- *Neck*
- *Chest*
- *Abdomen*

And work your way down as far as you want to go all the way to your feet if you would like. Then you will work backwards from your feet all the way back up to the top of your head or whatever starting point you have chosen.

You will take your hands and place them either on or right over the area you are working on. Hold them for a set length of time, two minutes seems to work great. You can use a small timer to track the time spent on each part of your body.

While you have your hands placed on or right above each area, focus on your breathing as well as whatever sensations you are feeling at the moment. If you finish one area but feel drawn to go back, repeat that area until you are comfortable removing your hands and moving on to the next area.

You want to do this for at least 3 to 4 months daily before ever practicing Reiki on someone else. Again you need to make sure you do this daily, I understand that there are times when you may not be able to fit in an entire session but some Reiki is better than no Reiki at all. If you can only focus on a few parts than make sure you focus on the ones you feel most drawn to. Either way, the Reiki energy is going to find the part of your body that it needs to work on at that moment.

While you are practicing Reiki on yourself, you will find that thoughts will come and go, allow them to but stay focused on your breathing, if a negative thought enters your mind, push it out and refocus. You may find that thoughts of what you have to accomplish that day or what bills need paid or even the random thought of what you need to purchase at the grocery store will try to creep into your mind, if it does let it pass, you can focus on those thoughts later but for now you need to be focused completely on balancing yourself.

As these thoughts enter your mind, just remind yourself that you are becoming balanced, you are healed and go back to focusing on your breath.

I have spoken to many people who have stated that in just one week of using self Reiki they have seen amazing changes in their lives. Some say that they just feel more positive and that they are able to think more clearly, others state they have become more productive and are much happier with life in general while still others say that in only a week they are seeing symptoms of health problems they have suffered with for years just disappear.

Before we go any farther, I want to make it clear that at no point should you quit taking any prescribed medications, it is okay to add some vitamins and minerals if a doctor says it is okay but until the doctor takes you off of your medications, continue taking them.

Printed in Great Britain
by Amazon.co.uk, Ltd.,
Marston Gate.